# JoAnn Dean,

*Self-Care for Success*

Reconnect. Reassess. Rise.

## A Woman's Guide To Understanding Her Value and Navigating Her Life With Confidence

Publisher's Cataloging-in-Publication data

Names: Dean, JoAnn, author.
Title: Self-care for success: a woman's guide to understanding her value and navigating her life with confidence / JoAnn Dean.

Description: Conyers, GA: Inspired By JoAnn, LLC, 2022.
Identifiers: LCCN: 2022911952 | ISBN: 978-0-9972519-1-3

Subjects: LCSH Self-care, Health. | Self-actualization (Psychology) in women. | Success. | Self-realization in women. | Women--Mental health. | Women--Conduct of life. | Self-help. | BISAC SELF-HELP / Personal Growth / Self-Esteem | SELF-HELP / Personal Growth / Happiness | SELF-HELP / Motivational & Inspirational

Classification: LCC HQ1206. D43 2022 | DDC 155.25--dc23

# Self-Care For Success

A Woman's Guide to Understanding Her Value and
Navigating Her Life with Confidence

**JoAnn S. Dean, MSW, BCC**

## Disclaimer

Although the author and publisher have made every effort to ensure the information in this book is correct at the press time, the author and publisher do not assume and hereby disclaim any liability to any party for any loss, damage, or disruption caused by error or omissions, whether such errors or omissions result from negligence, accident, or any other cause.

**Self-Care for Success** is a snapshot of my evolution.

I use writing to heal and help others. It's a part of my self-care plan. In "Self-Care for Success" I candidly share some of my journal entries mixed with coaching tools to aid the reader in reconnecting with who they are.

It is in our understanding of who we are, we can heal and build a stronger faith foundation. Our self-awareness gives us the courage to travel through life with confidence, experiencing evolution.

This very moment is connected to a generation.
What God is doing right now will follow us for years.
We are establishing a new identity and building a legacy.
God help us to be sensitive to how we're changing.

# Dedication

To my Godfather & Uncle Cleve, thank you for the space you filled. I wish we had more time. Rest in peace.

To Pops, thanks for being our rock. Rest in Peace.

Uncle AJ, thanks for being the MVP in my life.

Bobby, my big brother, I admire the man you are. Thank you for the spontaneous thoughtful gifts and timely talks.

Tommy, my brother, the quiet conqueror. Thank you for every yes.

Daniel, the cousin with a compassionate heart who always supports and cheers me on.

Alijah the musician, the godson who always delivers.

BJ, my youngest godson, thanks for choosing me. I got you.

Ronald, the friend who became my brother.

Michael, the cousin who always thought I was cool. Thanks for all the complimentary haircuts.

Ashton, my son, thanks for making me a bonus mom and Ladybug.

My father, thank you for the decision that created me. The lessons & the blessings your absence brought. Rest in Peace.

Dean, Bae, my hubby, my protector, my promise keeper. Thank you for loving me.

"The strength of a man is in his character. A strong man is a great man of wisdom who understands, his top priority is to his family."

— Ellen J. Barrie

Thank You!

# Self-care.

It's reflected in how we move, how we speak, how we interact with others, the boundaries we display and how we go throughout our days.

It's in our everyday walk, the vibration of our talk. Our laughter and tears, the generational patterns that's been on repeat for years.

Self-care speaks in our sleep, turn those thoughts off, stop them from playing on repeat. Your spirit wants to shine through offering you a seat with a different view.

It's frustrated because you've been playing too small. It's time to stand tall, rise and answer the call.

A generation is in need, you must believe, because it's your turn to lead. Lead them out of old traditions and into owning their positions. Oh yes, gifted indeed, they're here to fulfill a mission born out of a need.

Pick a path and release the past, you no longer need it. Lessons were learned, love was shared, now step into a higher calling if you dare. Go ahead step on the gas, you're prepared, this lifetime needs your unwavering care.

# HEALING IS A GIFT.

My hope is that you'll create rhythms of rest. Break behavior patterns that no longer serve you and create a legacy that out lives you.

# We should all have a self-care plan.

We are a spirit living in a body, and that body requires maintenance. Born with a beautiful intention, we were chosen to BE here at this precise moment in time. Consideration was carefully made for the curves that frame our bodies, the strength that secures our footing and the gifting to carry out our earthly missions.

The stunning beautiful shades of the skin we wear does a delightful dance as the sunlight finds its way in. Energized by its presence, seeking protection, and proudly standing guard of the inner workings buried beneath the surface a soul saturated with stories and strongholds stand at an entryway desiring to break free from the past, fighting its way through decades of dismay. Our spirit calls out for us to follow its lead, it knows the path, the way has been paved for our highest good, to feel more alive than we believed we ever would.

Becoming self-aware we declare, with every breath we take, and with every stride we make. We will break patterns of limiting beliefs and build bold bridges that connect us to a better way of living.

Our eyes, created to see beyond the basics and our ears eager to elevate their capacity to hear, deeply discerning the data flowing through life's database as we persevere.

Our heart, created to love and shed light, illuminating the path of others through our ability to serve at new heights. We're a masterpiece. We're fierce and we have been found favorable to carry out the mission that brought us here.

Our hands, they're blessed to work. To mold. To shape and create.

Our voice commands attention, it creates a detailed portrait of its vision, dressed up priorities on display, our words seek to master come what may. Words radically reflect our feelings and foundation, filling up spaces adding to each day, in some way reminders us of our ancestors who paved the way. The soft ones and the spirited ones, we underestimate their power, we casually speak to them, mindlessly murmuring as if their predictions won't take root, reaching deeply into the soil of a soul born for a different use. Every word is a prayer of creation. Its crafted and called out, manifested by the power we possess to create brighter pathways for future generations to confidently navigate their way and comprehend, the assignment is to transcend.

> **"Talk to yourself like you would to someone you love."**
>
> ~Brené Brown

# Forward

You are of great worth; you are powerful, and you are authentic. Your divine purpose ranges from giving birth, birthing ideas, and creating movements, to caring for those near the end of life, developing ideas to fruition, and propelling movements. Self-care is a foundational step to greatness. The best thing you can do for those you love and care about is to care for self. I often share with spouses the most important thing you can do for your relationship is to pray and care for your spouse's spouse. Without self-care, our light becomes dim and weak rendering us unable to light the path for others. Teaching our young to utilize their time and resources to care for themselves actively and socially is a gift to generations.

Self-care is an expression of self-love. So often we desperately want to love and care for others when we are unable to love and care for ourselves. As women, it is often the expectation of everyone to take care of them and all their needs and wants before yours. For some, it is a miss guided badge of honor to care for everyone except self. As women of color, we are falsely taught that we are uniquely made to be strong and not need the same care and love that all women need and deserve. As women of faith, we often struggle with the idea that taking care of self is selfish or ungodly, quite the contrary. As believers, we have been called to serve our purpose. Not called to a good feeling or a good idea but to serve a specific purpose designed by God for us.

"You are the salt of the earth; but if the salt should lose its flavor, how shall it be made salty again? It is no longer good for anything, except to be thrown out and trampled underfoot by men." Matthew 5:13.

Matthew 5 declares our need to be continually restored and renewed, in pursuit of self-care.

I honor and celebrate JoAnn Dean the author of Self-Care for Success, who has labored in this project to shine a light on the gift of self-care. Through this written project you have taught us lessons on how to show up in the world as our best authentic selves. Thank you for sharing your talent and insight with each of us.

*It is my prayer that God will continue to grow your amazing gift. To help you to always use your words to build up. Grant you all you need to bless others with your words. To be ever mindful of the power and magnitude of your words.*

May God Richly Bless You,
*Rev. BreNita Jackson*

# Let me introduce myself

I am Social Worker, Board Certified Life Coach and Writer.

I love empowering women to lead purposeful lives by focusing on the values of Self-Care, Spirituality and Self-Development to create what they define as success.

I offer a state of the heart experience inspiring professional women to discover and step into who they really are and navigate their lives with confidence.

When I relocated from New Orleans to Atlanta, I missed my girlfriends, my support system. I began hosting a small group of women at my home to connect and confide in one another. It was then that I realized how much we need a safe space to fellowship with like-minded women and reconnect with ourselves. This group blossomed into what is now known as an exclusive membership community called "The Faith Circle".

As a result of pouring into so many women, my first book was birthed, "It Begins With You" a journey of faith, forgiveness and how to move forward.

My path shifted when I became clear about who I am, what I valued, and how it impacted every area of my life.

Are you ready for your shift?

**Disruption** of the old necessitates discomfort as we step into the new. It all begins with our thoughts. The thoughts we choose to focus on; they shape our view. Disrupting unhealthy thought patterns is a form of self-care. This act of love causes us to look at ourselves in a new way.

It's one thing to want change and another to replace your current way of being with a system that serves you where you are and positions you for where you are headed. With any breakup there's a grief process. Letting go takes courage. Don't resist your ability to feel. The old you have value. She's brought you here. The past experiences were your teacher.

I'd been asking God to show me where I needed to grow. The conversations led to personal and spiritual growth. I'm an introvert who has been called to create. I see a sisterhood, strong and full of faith, still we need support to evolve into who we are with grace. As uncomfortable as it gets sometimes, to be out front, I am committed to doing my part. I'm showing up for me and holding space for you, together we will face our truth. The beautiful thing about our paths is God will provide what we need at each intersection of our lives. Now what we do with this provision is totally up to us.

What are you choosing for you?

I want us to become hungry for what's calling us. My prayer is we don't continue to hang our cute hats on being a strong woman, bragging about having to do it all. Instead, we exercise our ability to ask and receive. Asking God for strength and vision. Clarity and courage to crack the code and come out on the other side of what has us confined.

We're either going to operate from a place of fear or love. Don't allow fear to dictate your course.

It's time! It's time to step into all of you! The change must take place in you before it can fully flow into your community. When we experience change it creates a clearer path, in us and around us. Pray for me as I pray for you.

*"Sometimes I wake up & have to remind myself: "There is nothing wrong with me. I have patterns to unlearn, new behaviors to embody & wounds to heal. But there is nothing wrong with the core of me & who Iam. I am unlearning generations of harm and remembering love. It takes time." ~Yolo Akili*

To my sister on the path, the professional woman,

I am amazed how we can become frustrated when others break promises to us, yet we don't always keep the promises we make to ourselves. As women we give so much of ourselves, rarely pausing to replenish.

As professional women, we hold ourselves accountable to others. We set the bar high. We aim our thoughts and actions towards showing up in a way that serves others sometimes eliminating ourselves. The time has come to put yourself first. To reconnect with yourself. To reassess what you value and to rise and embrace all of who you are. I'm here to hold space for you as you navigate your new way of being.

**It's about being:**

P- positioned
R – reliable
O -on the ball
F -fierce
E -experienced
S -strategic
S -savvy
I -intuitive
O -original
N -nurturing
A -authentic
L -loyal to self

According to webster "A professional has been defined as one who engages in a specified activity as one's main or paid occupation rather than as a pastime."

**"If you are always trying to be normal, you will never know how amazing you can be."**

– Dr. Maya Angelou

# Allow Yourself

Allow yourself to dream,
And when you do dream big

Allow yourself to learn
And when you do learn all you can

Allow yourself to laugh
And when you do share your laughter

Allow yourself to set goals
And when you do reward yourself as you move forward

Allow yourself to be determined
And when you do you will find you will succeed

Allow yourself to believe in yourself
And when you do you will find self confidence

Allow yourself to lend a helping hand
And when you do a hand will help you.

Allow yourself relaxation
And when you do you will find new ideas.

Allow yourself love
And when you do you will find love in return

Allow yourself to be happy
And when you do you will influence others around you.

Allow yourself to be positive
And when you do life will get easier.

**by Catherine Pulsifer**

# Self-Care Commitment

I felt stuck for a portion of my life. Sometimes, I still find myself engaged in moments where I'm cleaning the tacky residue from the souls of my shoes. It is my commitment to self-care that keeps me on course, avoiding knee deep situations that sabotage my progress.

Experience has taught me as I help others, I help myself. Holding space for the professional women who hold space for everyone else is my priority. I welcome women into an intimate setting "The Inspired By JoAnn Community" where we learn new ways of relating to ourselves. Together we discover and integrate new blueprints for the women we are embracing.

JoAnn Dean, MSW, BCC

"Almost everything will work again if you unplug it for a few minutes, including you."

~ Anne Lamott

# Introduction

I was a couple of years out of graduate school working for the State of Louisiana. While attending a Rest & Relaxation training, this quote was a part of the welcome packet.

Our deepest fear is not that we are inadequate.
Our deepest fear is that we are powerful beyond measure.
It is our light, not our darkness
That most frightens us.
We ask ourselves
Who am I to be brilliant, gorgeous, talented, fabulous?
Actually, who are you not to be?
You are a child of God.
You're playing small
Does not serve the world.
There's nothing enlightened about shrinking
So that other people won't feel insecure around you.
We are all meant to shine,
As children do.
We were born to make manifest
The glory of God that is within us.
It's not just in some of us.
It's in everyone.
And as we let our own light shine,
We unconsciously give other people permission to
do the same.
As we're liberated from our own fear,
Our presence automatically liberates others.

**By Marianne Williamson**

I remember how empowered I felt after reading it, a layer of uncertainty and fear fell off me! I begin a deep dive into the root of my fear. For me, that included fasting and praying. While in this spiritual space the connection was revealed to me. When I was 5 years old, I was enrolled in school, first grade. One day without warning I was asked to pack up my things and I was escorted to the kindergarten side of the building where I would spend the remainder of the school year. This experience caused me to remain stuck for a great portion of my life, feeling boxed in and afraid to fully live. You see, because of this experience, I embraced the limiting belief I had to be perfect to be accepted. What this experience also taught me is our trauma can block our memory. My cousin and I started school together, although we were the same age, she got to stay in the first grade; however, someone reported my age didn't reflect my grade. And it didn't.

During a conversation with my cousin later in life, she shared after I was removed from the classroom, she spent many days crying. She recalled the teacher would come and get me, I would give her a pep talk and return to my classroom. At five, I was operating in purpose! I was already a Social Worker, a Life Coach, and an inspiration.

# Table of Contents

# Defining
# Self-Care

01

As you begin your journey of recommitting to self-care, I want to invite you to consider these three pillars as you carve out your own path. Remember to prioritize your needs minus the needs of others. Pivot when necessary and exercise patience with yourself.

**Prioritize** your needs.
**Pivot** as you go.
Exercise **patience** with yourself.

> "Love is the great miracle cure. Loving
> ourselves works miracles in our lives."
>
> ~Louise Hay

# Seek & You Shall Find

A prophetic session with a minister brought clarity and a new level of consciousness that called me higher.

He allowed the presence of God to guide him as he literally read me. Lol! The message was so spot on. I am thankful for his gift and his obedience to share it with so many. I left his presence feeling seen and heard for the first time in a long time. It served as a confirming message. I felt my Heavenly Father and my loving ancestors saying we see, and we know what you're made of, now activate it!

My grandmother, who I affectionately called Mother, reared me from birth. She had great expectations of me. It was evident by how she challenged me to "BE somebody" as she would say on many occasions. I realize now, me being somebody reflected the vision she had for her life. Her vision was to educate and graduate all of her children and position them for success. I recall after she read my first book. She said you did good. You're doing the things I was too shy to do. That is, you're sharing your writing and speaking in front of an audience. There are no words to capture how grateful I am she got to see me "BE somebody" this was her measurement of success. It was an incredible moment to witness her feel all the feelings that supported her vision of educating and graduating her children to position them for success.

As I pondered deeper into my spiritual work, the answers arrived. I had let others project their fear onto me. Once again, I had allowed the outside voices to be louder than mine, influencing my decision making. And now I am left wondering where I would be on my spiritual journey had I not allowed the external voices to override my spirit guide. Forgive me Lord. I see now, how I made the shift from being to feeling the need to build. I bought into all the cares of this world. I was always a person of faith even when I was too young to recognize it. My heightened sensitivity has always served and guided me.

The minister was used by God to reintroduce me to that part of me. It's been calling out to me, not just to return to me, but return and embrace the gifts and calling that's on my life.

What are you in search of?

4

# What is Self-Care

Self- care is not just about spa days, it also includes examining behavior patterns we do not want to pass down as a part of our legacy. Self-care is taking the time to do things that help us live well and improve our physical, mental, and spiritual health.

After my grandmother's transition in 2018, as a part of my self-care, I hired a wellness coach to hold space for me while I processed and moved through what I was feeling. I didn't want to live in the grief as I had done in the past with my sister's passing. While the grief process is different for each of us and it takes as long as it takes, this was the best decision for me.

Through my business, Inspired By JoAnn, LLC, the priority is holding space for the professional women who holds space for everyone else. Without our mental health intact, we cannot manifest the life we desire.

"Mental Health includes our emotional, psychological, and social well-being. It affects how we think, feel, and act. It also helps determine how we handle stress, relate to others, and make healthy choices. Mental health is important at every stage of life, from childhood and adolescence through adulthood". -CDC

With this book, my intention is to empower the reader to take a closer look at their current self-care plan. I share what my deeper dive into self-care helped me to discover and the patterns I'm healing and breaking. I face my shadow self. This is the part of us hidden from our own awareness and is usually experienced through relationships.

I invite you to extend unconditional love and compassion to yourself as you walk the path identifying old patterns that no longer serve you. Give yourself permission to heal while honoring who you are.

**"Our legacy depends on us taking care of ourselves."**

# How To Practice Self-Care

"Self-Care isn't a matter of having time, it's a matter of readjusting what you do with the time you have."

Committing to self-care is an important part of building a healthier version of you. It's a way to connect with the deeper parts of you. Practicing self-care helps with preventing and recovering from burnout. It aids in improving sleep patterns and relationships. How we treat ourselves displays how we feel about ourselves, and it teaches others how to treat us.

**Ways to Practice:**

Self-Awareness (get to know who you are)

Make healthier food choices

Get Enough Sleep

Move Regularly

Declutter your space

Set Boundaries

Forgive Yourself

Forgive Others

Find Ways to Relax

Check-In with Yourself

Connect with Others

**"We can only take people as far as we have gone ourselves."**

"The greatest legacy one can pass on to one's children and grandchildren is not money, but rather a legacy of character and faith."

~ Billy Graham

# Benefits of
# Self-Care

## O2

# Benefits of Self-Care

It is essential for managing stress and preventing burnout.
- It offers a sense of overall integrity, as it ensures we are "walking our talk"
- It boosts self-esteem.
- It is an opportunity to focus on yourself, taking time to rest, reflect, replenish, and renew.
- It protects your mental health.
- It's a time to take stock of your own needs, goals, health, and accomplishments.
- It's about nourishing and nurturing all of who you are.
- It doesn't just affect you; it spills over onto those you love.

# Self-Care Check In

It's okay to put yourself first.

What does self-care mean to you?

_____

_____

How do you currently practice self-care?

_____

_____

How are you managing your feelings?

_____

_____

What are you not experiencing right now that you want to experience?

_____

_____

**Understanding who you are is the foundation for a Successful Self-Care Plan.**

"Let go of past version of yourself, even if it's positive."

# Self-Awareness

Self-awareness is defined as having a clear perception of your personality, including strengths, weaknesses, thoughts, beliefs, motivation, and emotions. Self-awareness allows you to understand other people and how they perceive you, your attitude, and your response to them.

**How self-aware are you?**

It's time to face your shadow self. This is the part of you that is hidden from your own awareness and is usually experienced through relationships. What old patterns are you judging? I invite you to become willing to extend unconditional love and compassion to yourself as you heal from what no longer serves you and step into who you truly are.

*What does your name mean?*

A name connects us to our soul. It provides us with spiritual ammunition, allowing us to access spiritual strengths we may have never known we had.

*What's your Love Language?*

Dr. Gary Chapman wrote "The 5 Love Languages" in 1992. The term "love languages" explains the fundamentally different ways we express and receive love. The Love Languages are also used in business.

The five love languages are five different ways of expressing and receiving love:
- Words of affirmation
- Quality time
- Receiving gifts
- Acts of service
- Physical touch

*What's your Communication Style?*

Communication styles are different approaches to expressing our thoughts, feelings, and opinions. "Based upon the work of William M. Marston, often referred to as DISC, the **HRDQ Style Model** provides a simple and powerful framework that learners can apply to how they communicate, lead others, manage time, learn, coach, and sell."

Which style do you feel best describes you?

**DIRECT**

- Gets to the bottom line
- Speaks forcefully
- Maintains eye contact
- Presents position strongly

**SPIRITED**

- Persuasive
- A good storyteller
- Focuses on the big picture
- Uses motivational speech

**CONSIDERATE**

- Listens well
- Is a good counselor
- Uses supportive language
- Builds trust

**SYSTEMATIC**

- Presents precisely
- Focus on facts
- Efficient on speech
- Well organized workplace

| What's your Personal Mission? |
| --- |

A personal mission statement defines who you are as a person (or as a team member where you work) and identifies your purpose, whether that's in the office or simply in life. It explains how you aim to pursue that purpose, and why it matters so much to you.

Ex. "To use my gifts and talents to improve the lives of others."

| What do you Value? |
| --- |

Your *values* are the things you believe are important about your life. Those values inform your decision making and drives your behavior. They help you to remain focused on what's important to you.  When you are clear about what you value, it's easier to say no to distraction and those things that do not align with your path.

| What's your Skillset? |
| --- |

The meaning of **SKILL SET** is a collection of skills and abilities that can be applied to a professional or creative endeavor. In determining your skillset, look at what you do daily. What trainings have you participated in, formal or informal? Also ask those you trust what they see in you. Your skills could have come from many places, it all counts.

"Self-love means having a high regard for your own well-being and happiness. Self-love means taking care of your own needs and not sacrificing your well-being to please others."

# Who Are You?

**My name is**_____
and it means _____

My **love language** is_____
My **communication style** is _____

My **personal mission statement**
is_____

_____

I **value**_____
and _____

My **skills** include_____
and _____

Why these things matter? It can help you stay focused, happy,
healthy, and resilient!

"Carve your name on hearts, not tombstones. A legacy is etched into the minds of others and the stories they share about you."

~ Shannon Adler

# Creating a Personalized Self-Care Plan

03

# Self-Care Success Plan of Action

A **self-care plan** is a "thoughtfully constructed and intentionally engaged wellness guide to promote our health and well-being."

**Please take a moment and fill in the blanks with what you will commit to do for yourself.**

**Daily** I will

_____

**Weekly** I will

_____

**Monthly** I will

_____

**Quarterly** I will

_____

## Well Done!
You've created a self-care plan that serves you.
Now, add yourself to your calendar and make it non-negotiable.

For us to become whole and healthy, we must balance the body, mind, and spirit. We need to take good care of our bodies. We need to have a positive attitude about ourselves and about life. And we need to have a strong spiritual connection.

~Louise Hay

## Asking Empowering Questions

"Empowering questions are **open-ended, thought-provoking, challenging, and solution-oriented questions that cause a person to search for answers and new possibilities.**"

# Defining Self-care Moments (My Evolution)

O4

"Don't forget to appreciate yourself.
~Mridha

# The Journal of JoAnn

What I know for sure. On any given day you will experience a different part of me. I am uncovering, discovering, healing and highlighting all of who I am.

I will mess up.
I will rise to the occasion.
I will say something I want to take back.
I will experience the power of my words at work in someone else's life.
I will cry.
I will laugh.
I will experience pain.
I will enjoy pleasure.
I will question my abilities.
I will use the affirming words of others to step higher into who I am.
I will be misunderstood.
I will misunderstand.
I will eat.
I will fast.
I will lose.
I will gain.
I will celebrate others.
I will be celebrated.
I will rest.
I will rise.
I will passionately express myself.
I will purposely pause.
I will remember the words of others.
I will share memorable messages.
I will express gratitude.
I will receive gratitude.
I will extend forgiveness.
I will be forgiven.
I am spirit.
I am human.
I am the dream of my ancestors.
I am becoming.
I am complete.

# **Decluttering** is the act of removing unnecessary items.

Decluttering serves as a part of my self-care and mindset renewal, while I casually move towards a minimalist way of being.

Letting go and reassess value created space for a new way of being. Releasing was the gateway for me to be completely honest with myself and those around me about who I am stepping into and where my loyalty lies.

Every self-care moment connects me with my higher self. It's an ongoing process of getting to know who I am, what I value & the value I bring. It's recognizing what season I'm in and owning who I am! It's having the courage to take full responsibility for my life without the permission of others to Be me!

I believe there is a place where we all fit perfectly into God's divine plan. Things get messy when we negate the responsibility of being who we are. We become the missing piece. We open the door for confusion and self-doubt allowing the famously known imposter syndrome to take up rent free residency. Now each day reflects decisions of desperation because we're battling the mental madness of being out of position, muddling through feelings of misrepresentation. The way back is to reconnect with ourselves and embrace the spiritual work of understanding what we believe.

Our faith is important because we build based on what we believe. What we believe leads us to more abundance of that belief.

Letting go of things and narratives that once served as a protective barrier when we needed it, knowing who we are, what we value and the value we bring is a key ingredient for increasing our confidence in life and businesses.

If your heart is desiring something different, just for today, give yourself permission to consider who you are? What you believe? And where your faith lies?

# Reflections

# Movement Moves Emotions

As I strolled down the intentionally designed path in Midtown Atlanta accompanied by a friend, in between pondering shared thoughts and reflections, I couldn't help but notice God's beauty all around as I appreciated the sunshine that bathe my face on this brisk morning. It was my self-care time. Movement moves our emotions and releases endorphins. This exchange has always felt miraculous to me.

Miracles—both big and small—are all around us. We stand in anticipation of the massive, magnificent miracle to be performed in our lives, yet sometimes we miss the small spectacular ones along the way. If I am focused on what I don't have I'll surely miss what God is doing around me, in me, and through me. Should God come in with His majestic wand and completely heal us of whatever ails us in this moment? If He chooses to, you best believe your girl will praise Him for that! But, if He requires some work on our part, let's make the effort He's calling us to make. Successful people don't leave their change up to chance.

Things occur in our lives every day that should bend our knees in gratitude, compelling us to express how grateful our heart is to God.

Pause for a minute- reflect on the gift of self-awareness. There are many things we're aware of that perhaps we take for granted: relationships, rewarding work, financial provision, family---the one given to us at birth and the one we've chosen to create.

Let's not forget the ability to simple care for ourselves and choose what we decide to put in and, on our bodies, and the very air we're privileged to breathe. Oh, how much we take for granted some days.

There are also many things that are beyond our vision, and we have no idea they're in play. We don't know everything God has spared us from, but rest assured, He has. Being self-aware is a form of self-care

.

# Reflections

# Sandwiched in Between

My birthday is January 13th.

Birthday celebrations are not what they used to be. I find myself as the year comes to an end, bracing myself for the flood of memories of my grandmother's transition. 21 days to be exact. Her transition illuminated my path. Clarity about past lingering questions was gained and a spiritual consciousness was cracked open.

I'm sandwiched in between my two angels. My sister's born day was January 10th. My grandmother's born day was January 26th, and her transition date was January 21st. which began on News Years Day. There's been 11 heavenly birthday celebrations for my sister and 4 for my grandmother. Mines have been a blur. 11 has been a reoccurring number in my life over the past year. There are things that now serve as a teacher to me, that I hadn't given much attention to before. I see and hear differently. I credit the Holy Spirit for being my guide and comforter and I celebrate my ancestors for their shoulders and protection.

In a round of questions, I was recently asked "what do I take for granted?" I continued to ponder that question days later. And in this moment, I would add to my answer- all those who have gone before me and the sacrifices they made. If I'm honest, I've been dwelling on a level that's beneath my capacity. My grandmother's transition ignited me in a way I hadn't anticipated. I found myself wanting to check in on her after she departed this life. I know that sounds silly. I just wanted to know she made it to the other side safely and what her experience was like as she traveled to the next dimension: reuniting with loved ones and meeting her Heavenly Father.

There is an empowering shift that has taken place inside of me. It's a spiritual call to travel higher. As the spiritual door cracked open for me to gain entry, I asked for permission to step inside. New teachers have begun showing up. They have given me insight as I connect the dots from my past to this present moment. Our ancestors were robbed of their value, traditions, and rituals. And the extremely sad part about it is we continue to be brainwashed about who we are and the power we possess. We were taught our traditions and rituals are taboo while other races are packaging and profiting off what was originally ours!

For the past several years I have found myself with a strong desire to unplug from the world as much as possible every October. I'm encouraged to get quiet and seek God for where my focus should go for the upcoming year. Our discussion always begins with a word.

In 2019- Rebirth.

In 2020 – Vision.

In 2021- Reintroduction.

In 2022- Bloom

I've been reborn, my vision is clearer, and I've been reintroduced to myself and God.

In my current season of BLOOMING, I'm appearing more attractive, becoming more confident and successful to myself. My grandmother always wanted me to "BE somebody". I believe it was her way of measuring success, her sacrifice. I believe the best way to honor her is to BE my authentic self and we both win.

My sister would always say, "Don't worry about it. It's okay". How could I not succeed and not be okay, with these two angels watching over me. One to my left and the other to my right, standing guard of their favorite girl.

37

# Titles limit our expansion

The title wife, was something I always imagined, prayed for, hoped for, believed for. That's why I was caught completely off guard when my spirit guide revealed to me it was the thing that caused me to shrink, second guess myself and stumble for a season of my life.

I was so focused on getting it right, I'd lost sight of who I was. This title and my church upbringing had me believing I had to become someone different to fulfill the mission as a wife. I noticed how much my energy had shifted and I no longer felt safe being me. The shrinkage I was experiencing fueled me with an internal rage. The thought of exchanging my dreams and desire to submit to another was unsettling to say the least. Resentment capped off my anger. The more I internalized my feelings of loss the more detached I was becoming from everyone and everything around me.

My saving grace was and is my relationship with my creator, my Heavenly Father. Even when I felt I was going through a dark night of my soul experience, God surrounded me with His love. And in a way only He could, He revealed me to me. He positioned divine connections on my path. He had people reach out to me for help that ended up helping me see me differently. I even experienced the loss of loved ones that served as my teacher. The loss of loved ones, opportunities and community pushed me into a space where there was no escaping confronting what had brought me here. Me My trauma triggers. My thinking. My limiting beliefs. My lack of communication. My desire to be perfect vs being me.

Has your title limited your expansion?

# Reflections

"The need to leave a legacy is our spiritual need to have a sense of meaning, purpose, personal congruence, and contribution."

– Stephen Covey

# Forgiven, yet triggered.

Some may say it's not a big deal, but I say I've missed out on and broken deals because of it. It has shown up in ways I didn't anticipate. More recently, it's shown up in the form of anger, an internal rage. All the unanswered questions, the searches that yielding no returns. The wondering about what parts of him reflects who I am. I'm speaking of the absence of my biological father.

I remember in my later teen years he showed up in my life for the first time. There he was standing on our front porch expecting entry. I don't know how or why but I knew who he was. Before any attempt of an introduction. I refused to engage in conversation with him. My grandmother encouraged me to give him a chance, but my heart wasn't ready. I remember thinking I didn't need him now; I had my grandparents. Plus, where had he been?! I felt abandoned and rejected. I had often wondered why I was the one without a dad.

Whenever I would inquire, my grandmother's reply was don't worry, I am your mom and dad. You will always have what you need. And she made sure of it. I don't remember ever wanting something and not receiving it. I am forever grateful for her.

Every so often the desire to understand this degree of separation would arise. Nothing could fill its space. My grandmother shared stories of his family's acceptance of me and how his mother would send a birthday cake every year even though it was clear she wasn't a baker. Lol. She said I resembled her. She loved hosting family gatherings and having a good time. I was too young to remember.

My grandmother introduced me to God. Because of her, my faith is my foundation. As I grew spiritually, I understood the importance of forgiveness. I remember talking to God about it and one of my college professors who I had begun to spend time with. She was good at challenging my thought process. I needed to forgive him, so I did. Even in my forgiveness I can see how his absence impacted me. I have had moments of struggling with abandonment issues, commitment issues and worthiness. But I fight the desire to blame or remain stuck in any of it. Because of my faith foundation, my upbringing, my education, and divine connections on my path I had the tools to continue moving forward.

An encounter with a minister challenged me, asking why I was feeling stuck, unsafe, and angry. I know this was him hearing from God. I was able to take a deep spiritual dive into what I was feeling, connecting the dots, leading me on a path to return to the soil where it all began. While sitting on the same porch my father stood on, my uncle's words gave me the masculine affirming I didn't know I needed. His words powerfully cut the cord that would only permit me to step so far into my destiny. I could even here my father say, even though I wasn't there it wasn't because of you. It was because of me. You are worthy and you lack nothing.

# Reflections

# Endings & New Beginnings

A recent conversation with my uncle was exactly what my soul needed. There were many words spoken and unspoken in the front yard where we grew up. The backdrop was picture perfect. As the sun shined brightly and the breeze seem to blow at the moment when it was most needed, we reflected on past memories and the experiences that brought us here.

While my Uncle cut the grass and tilled the soil to make room for his plans of adding new flowers to each of the flower beds positioned on each side of the steps leading up to the porch, he joked about my engagement in this process. As the conversation ascended to new heights, I moved from standing near the gate protecting the land my great grandfather purchased many years ago, to sitting on the steps after the sun had dried the remains of the water residue from the hose, he had used to shower debris from the porch. As if in a spiritual sync I moved from the steps to inside of the home once occupied by my grandmother who nurtured us both as siblings. I couldn't remember the last time these walls had graced me with their presence. If I'm honest, in the days approaching my visit home, this moment had occupied much of my headspace. How would I feel? What would I be thinking? How apparent would her presence be? As I crossed over the sill of the door, the floor didn't feel as sturdy as it once did. I wondered if it could still support me. Its pulse was different. It was calm. I was accustomed to the pressure, the high impact of our home where diamonds were made and expected to shine. It was always filled with productive activity.

I sensed a strong connection to the old hovering over me. As I entered further and gently sat on the love seat to my left, still positioned under the window, a desire to release the old spoke softly and strongly commanded me to fulfill the new. As my eyes continued to scan the room that reflected a museum image of her items just the way she'd left them, my gaze landed on the chair, a tan recliner. A retractable cane laid across it. I stood, walked a few steps across the floor and picked it up. My heart knew this was the piece of her that would return to Atlanta with me to accompany me on my walks.

I took another look around the room as if taking in a final moment in time before moving onto the next, breaking a barrier of some sort. As I pushed the screen door open and stepped back onto the porch, I found my uncle still at work and play. The sound of the screen door signaled my reappearance. He looked up at me and could not believe what I was holding. As I sat on the top step, he beamingly shared a 1 am experience surrounding the cane. As he spoke, I felt the vibrational connection between us and "Mother" rise, confirming her presence and approval of who we are and continue to Be.

I couldn't help but admire the rose bush smiling back at me. I gently removed a few of the roses from it. My grandmother loved her garden. My hands are now in one of her favorite places. The branches were beginning to exceed its boundary inside of the gate. I'm hearing her say y'all push the boundaries. She did that oh so well. Eleven (11) roses would return to Atlanta with me.

Noticing the time, we made another heart exchange as I departed to pick up my mom to visit my sister and uncle's gravesites. Afterwards, we joined some family members for a dinner hosted by a cousin I always desire to support. Immediately upon my arrival, my high vibration sinked quickly. Like water the joy flowed out of me. I no longer felt in sync with my highest self. All I could think of was wanting to return to the front porch of my grandmother's house in the company of my uncle, where his words nurtured and filled me like a bowl of her gumbo. This moment had become my greatest teacher.

What or who do you need to release?

# Reflections

"Remember to remember."
~A.J

# Life on Layaway

It's four in the morning and my thoughts are on repeat. These thoughts are here spilling all the tea. The story must change for me to grow. The direction is clear, though the path unsure.

The ebbs and flows, the highs and lows, the happy highlights and the shadows that seem to grow; grand or small it's my attention they seek, to seamlessly summons me.

Stand at attention they say, follow our lead, we know the way.

It'll shed light on your day. There's no doubt about it, your time is here. You must step into its flow releasing all fear.

What if you believed it's truth? You have a heart to serve and a gift of design, to produce beyond your capacity to maintain its fruit.

What if you placed the uncertainties on layaway? Leaving the unclaimed ticket that once took up significant space. On hold, the garments once appearing to be your size and style were a misrepresentation of who you were for a short while.

You've traded in the anxiety to live in alignment. Believing He made you precious and ready for every assignment, stronger than your circumstances, wiser than your weary thinking, more creative than the capacity to control where the content takes you.

Feeling the rhythm of your heartbeat rise, your spirit guide says it's time to fly, a fierce desire now burns inside, receipts dissolved, caution cancelled, the essence of evolution is all that's mentioned.

Our abilities and opportunities may differ, but rest assured we're all here on a mission. Throw away the layaway tickets. Cash in the concerns. You're being called higher because you're here to serve.

Feel for the flow of the current in your life. Follow it. Fill up on it and serve from its satisfying stream because you are the dream.

What's the fierce desire burning inside of you?

# Reflections

# Inner Conflict

I want to work, rest says no. We'll hold space for you as you walk through an alternate door.

The inner conflict is real. My heightened sensitivity desires a different meal. A platter of self-care and success, server you can hold the rest. My mind craves to speak, my hands are hungry to write. This hearty appetite is a buffet eaters delight.

The car is packed, gas tank on full, the hotel is booked and now hubby is giving me the look.

The weather is sunny, sky dancing in shades of blue, it feels as if the stage has been set for us two.

A meditative drive, consciousness on high, exploring unseen sights, green meadows and walks through the night.

Inspiration ignited, new messages coming through , a new getaway has opened just for you.

Rest is key. Kindness is a cure. Pausing for a purpose helps the heart to endure.

"Women need real moments of solitude and self-reflection to balance out how much of ourselves we give away." - Barbara De Angelis

# Ancestors in the Outfield

The way grieving shows up always takes us by surprise. The sorrow fills us up and leaks out when we least expect, giving us no time to take cover or create a disguise.

A casual conversation, a movie, a team sport, an inside joke, a favorite snack, can release a flood of memories, opening the doorway to a staircase filled with silence and a sensitive mood leading us on a path designed to dictate our next move.

These memories, the tears, they reflect unfinished feelings, they're expressions of the depth of care we couldn't find the words to communicate.

Our soul feels buried with its own concern. We're looking for new ways of being without their physical presence, leaning on the spirit to show support and make it all better.

Oh my love, cast your worries away, rest assure they feel you and hear you every day. They're with you and their divine presence surrounds you, they're saying they want to help you.

The pain will subside, your heartbeat will find a new rhythm. Its melody will inspire a delicate divine dance serving as a reunion. With the clapping of your hands and the melody takeover, if you let this movement take you higher, it will mesmerize you.

This divine beat will lift you up beyond your thoughts, surrounding you by all the players who've kept you on point. We're all here they say, we're your angels in the outfield and we're here to stay. So, turn the music up, let it heal you in every way, trust us when we say, we're only a conversation away.

# NOLA Living

Born to believe and express our creativity, the arts heal our hearts, ignite our faith elevating us to an awakened state.

With our heads held high we believe we can touch the sky. Reconnecting to what feels true, feeling aligned and brand new.

Our souls rejoice, second lines fill the streets, no one is a stranger as we all meet and greet.

Seafood boils, spade games too, and if we're lucky we'll hit a scratch off or two. Hurricane drinks and seasons too, nothing matches us coming together to support you.

The vibe is right, we take it through the night. Class becomes common, fun becomes fierce, these are memories that will last for the years.

# Changes

Its the 7th month and the 7th book, it has given me a new look. Self-care for Success it's the vibe for me. It's the ticket for admission, you just wait and see.

This year has been one of many changes. My path paved the way for profound healing and a deeper understanding. I embrace all the changes, big and small: God knows what's best and when I need rest.

Mind, body and spirit all growing roots with the aim of bearing the best fruit. Intentionally blooming in my season, because I'm called if for no other reason.

I'm feeling aligned, and my wings are in full spread as I take flight in anticipation of what lies ahead.

My days look different my conversation has changed. I'm on a mission to help heal lives and rewrite stories: to leave a trail of signs and wonders, igniting supreme glory.

We're born to do great things and bring about change. Legacy living. Legacy leaving. Trust me everything has meaning.

Honor who you are, even with your scars, they possess power and are filled with purpose. Your life is sacred!

Too many Sacrifices to count or take for granted- the time has come for you to produce on this planet.

# Dream State

I had a dream and in each scene the messages channeled healing. Side by side as we walked through the crowd, each smile shared new meaning.

Words of encouragement and confirmation saturated the scene, as glimmers of hope beautifully beamed.

Thank you so much, voices proclaimed, through the fingers cupped across the huge smiles slightly covering the corners of their eyes wide gaze.

This is incredible, this word feels just for me. Only God knew it would set me free.

Restored, hopeful, clarity has turned the key. The door is cracked open, the path is paved, courage is calling, a light illuminates the way.

I hear my inner voice saying let's go, sacrifices were made for us to shine brighter than those who came before. We have an obligation to do our part, time is too precious not to take part.

We're all important, all connected: the impact is greater when we celebrate our blessings.

# Confidence
# Builders

# Boldly Build Your Confidence

For you created my inmost being you knit me together in my mother's womb. I praise you because I am fearfully and wonderfully made; your works are wonderful; I know that full well. ~Psalm 139:13-14

So, we say with confidence, "The Lord is my helper; I will not be afraid. What can mere mortals do to me?" ~Hebrews 13:6

So do not fear, for I am with you; do not be dismayed, for I am your God. I will strengthen you and help you; I will uphold you with my righteous right hand. ~Isaiah 41:10

Have I not commanded you? Be strong and courageous. Do not be afraid; do not be discouraged, for the LORD your God will be with you wherever you go." ~Joshua 1:9

This is the confidence we have in approaching God: that if we ask anything according to his will, he hears us. ~John 5:14

And being confident of this, that he who began a good work in you will carry it on to completion until the day of Christ Jesus. ~Philippians 1:6

I can do all this through him who gives me strength. ~Philippians 4:13

Let us then approach God's throne of grace with confidence, so that we may receive mercy and find grace to help us in our time of need. ~Hebrews 4:16

So do not throw away your confidence; it will be richly rewarded. You need to persevere so that when you have done the will of God, you will receive what he has promised. ~Hebrews 10: 35-36

# What is the will of God?

Do not be conformed to this world, but be transformed by the renewal of your mind, that by testing you may discern what is the will of God, what is good and acceptable and perfect. ~Romans 12:2

Give thanks in all circumstances; for this is the will of God in Christ Jesus for you. ~1 Thessalonians 5:18

Trust in the Lord with all your heart, and do not lean on your own understanding. In all your ways acknowledge him, and he will make straight your paths. ~Proverbs 3:5-6

But seek first the kingdom of God and his righteousness, and all these things will be added to you. ~Matthew 6:33

For God gave us a spirit not of fear but of power and love and self-control. ~ 2 Timothy 1:7

Have I not commanded you? Be strong and courageous. Do not be frightened, and do not be dismayed, for the Lord your God is with you wherever you go." ~ Joshua 1:9

Delight yourself in the Lord, and he will give you the desires of your heart. ~Psalm 37:4

And whatever you ask in prayer, you will receive, if you have faith." ~ Matthew 21:22

For nothing will be impossible with God." ~Luke 1:37

# Warrior Weapons

According to Webster, a warrior is someone who understands their needs and is fearless in telling others what they are, even at the risk of being vulnerable. A warrior is fearless in living. A warrior knows their gifts and develops them throughout their life.

As believers we have been given tools (warrior weapons) to fight against those things that would attempt to rob us of our God given birth rights.

Those weapons include:
- The word of God
- The Holy Spirit
- Communion
- Community
- Meditation
- Worship
- Prayer

A warrior knows suffering and still chooses to act with courage.

# Self-Care Success:
# The Evidence

O6

"If you don't love yourself, nobody will. Not only that, you won't be good at loving anyone else. Loving starts with the self."

—Wayne Dyer

I didn't realize this, but after working with JoAnn it was made evident that I had lost trust in myself. She guided me through personal and spiritual inquiry that brought to light what, why and how to my losing my way. She created a truly non-judgmental and thought-provoking space that helped me reinvigorate my clarity of professional purpose and direction. I am truly grateful as I look forward to future endeavors. ~ *S. Jackson, Registered Dietician*

---

**"This VIP Session helped me to get Unstuck, gain clarity and move in the direction of my dream."**

I'm a business owner who had a vision but felt stuck. This VIP Session helped me to get Unstuck, gain clarity and move in the direction of my dream. JoAnn was patient and compassionate while asking questions that served as a guide, helping me to identify the blocks that were preventing me from moving forward.

Through this process I was able to release these emotional blocks and create a step-by-step plan to create the life and business plan I had envisioned. ~ *M. Knight, Grief Coach & Educator*

Though I didn't think it was for me, I was blessed by the very first Faith Circle meeting. The warm welcome and no judgment zone let me know I was free to BE me. I didn't have to be Lady Bea, the Pastor's wife of Madea. I could be Beatrice Jones, free to speak. The atmosphere was filled with love. I loved it so much I invited friends and coworkers to attend future events. The circle reminded me I wasn't the only person going through experiences. The encouragement and safety leave me in anticipation of our next in person event after this pandemic passes.

*~ Lady B. Jones*

---

You have always motivated me to reach higher and never give up.

*~Chi Chi*

---

What a pleasure this was for me to connect with JoAnn. She is such a powerful woman of God. Her heart for ministry is evident in her smile and in her compassionate work for God's kingdom.

*~S. Busby*

# I have nothing but praise…...

When I first heard of how awesome you are and the powerful work you do, I was at a Vision Board party and my friend stood in the middle of the room and proclaimed how wonderful your book is and how you helped her navigate her life, especially after the tragic death of her son. Her testimony moved me. At that moment I was in a state of despair, feeling unworthy, afraid to step into my greatness...I was stuck. So instead of going on a food binge or a shopping spree, I called you. So glad I did! You helped so much.

I had huge negative self-talk and compared myself to others. You began by simply having me set up a schedule, that worked for me. I started going back to the gym, increasing water intake and I lost 10 lbs. and I'm still counting! When it came to my business, I will admit, I was hesitant to go there. You asked me write one sentence to explain my business, I was "stuck". I sat down and worked it out. Things began to come together!

I have nothing but praise for what you do for people JoAnn, getting people to take that little step forward, until we feel like we can bounce ahead and be ok. I will forever be grateful for your help and setting me in the right direction. ~Shae

I decided in 2020 to enhance my life for the better by enrolling in coaching services through Inspired By JoAnn, LLC. JoAnn tailored each session for my specific needs and goals. Her coaching truly changed my approach to life by offering me tools and methods to move out of my comfort area to where I wanted to be.

She comes highly recommended because of her detailed nature and her endless concerns for her clients. She is effective in helping you to achieve a fresh perspective and goal setting in real time. She taught me techniques and strategies that were simple to implement while holding me accountable for the work. *~Dr. Wyatt*

---

I was always able to take something back I learned from each event. The Faith Circle is a safe place for me to refill. Each event was always on time for where I was in life. There were so many gems given throughout each session that impacted my personal and spiritual journey. *~B. Johnson*

You challenged me to ask myself the difficult questions and helped me to see me for who I am. I admire who you are and all that you pour into others. Words cannot capture how much you mean to me and the Faith Circle. *~V. Wilburn, Certified Accountant*

---

Joining "The Faith Circle" was right on time for me. It fits me because I can be both, my personal and professional self, without judgement. The Faith Circle provides more than one can imagine. What some would consider a meeting, I feel it as a weekly get-together with sister friends. Each week brings something different, a new view, thought, an ah-ha or even an oh no moment. It is spirit lead and spirit fed - what a winning combination. *~J. Jones*

Our culture has us programmed to think that we cannot support one another as sisters, only to believe that we need to continue to run around like a hamster on a wheel figuring it out by ourselves; however, this is entirely erroneous. I have received a surplus of support from my Faith Circle during this transformative healing journey during this season of my life. I have been allowed to share my vulnerabilities without being judged or ridiculed. I am indebted to my Faith Circle sisters for the love and support I have received during my journey and hold a genuine appreciation and gratitude for the network established. JoAnn, thank you for being obedient and following the path presented to you. Know that the community you have created for women that need a safe space to be allowed to be vulnerable, transparent and heal what ails us all will remain under the grit of the highest and forever blessed beyond our most visionary expectations. *~R. Henderson, LCSW*

**"I have received a surplus of support from my Faith Circle Family during this transformative healing journey during this season of my life."**

"As you grow older, you will discover that you have two hands, one for helping yourself, the other for helping others."

— Maya Angelou

# Self-Discovery through Journaling

## A 7 Day Journey

**O7**

# Using Silence as a Skill

The introvert in me learned to use silence as a skill. While carving out space to journal and commune with God, unimaginable doors opened.

My journal serves as my receipt. It helps me prioritize my concerns, visualize my fears, reduce my stress, identify my self-talk, and channel my creativity, all while connecting the dots to clarity. This insight served as the vehicle for creating strategies that helped me to breakthrough and build a life that reflects the legacy I am living!

As a result of my deep spiritual dive and the power of journaling, I've learned what motivates me, inspires me, triggers me, and serves me as I serve others. Writing is a gift I've come to embrace. Writing is a place of comfort for me. It is in my being still and silent I've come to know.

I encouraged you to journal about what you are feeling. Then create a God list. Why, because He has promised to perfect the things that concerns us. And time and time again He has.


Unleash your giant through journaling!

# The Benefits of Journaling
(According to Kaiser Permanente)

"What do Albert Einstein, Marie Curie, Frida Kahlo, Leonardo da Vinci, and Frederick Douglass all have in common? Each of these famous figures kept a journal or diary to record their experiences, thoughts, or feelings.

Sometimes negative thoughts and emotions can run on a loop in our heads. This can be stressful when you're dealing with a challenging situation — it can even make your present situation feel worse. But if you stop and put your emotions down on paper, it can help you release negative thoughts from your mind. As you write, you may even come up with a solution you hadn't thought of before."

**Journaling:**
- helps to reduce stress.
- promotes health and well-being.
- helps you escape negative thoughts.
- provides a way to process emotions.
- help you figure out your next step.
- deepens self-discovery.

# *What's my God List?*

_____
_____
_____
_____
_____
_____
_____
_____
_____
_____
_____
_____
_____
_____
_____
_____
_____
_____
_____
_____
_____
_____
_____
_____
_____
_____
_____
_____
_____
_____
_____
_____
_____
_____
_____

# *How do I want to feel?*

# *What's missing in my life?*

# *What am I putting off?*

# *What am I telling myself about myself?*

# *What am I afraid of?*

# *How do I know I am ready to change?*

_____
_____
_____
_____
_____
_____
_____
_____
_____
_____
_____
_____
_____
_____
_____
_____
_____
_____
_____
_____
_____
_____
_____
_____
_____
_____
_____
_____
_____
_____

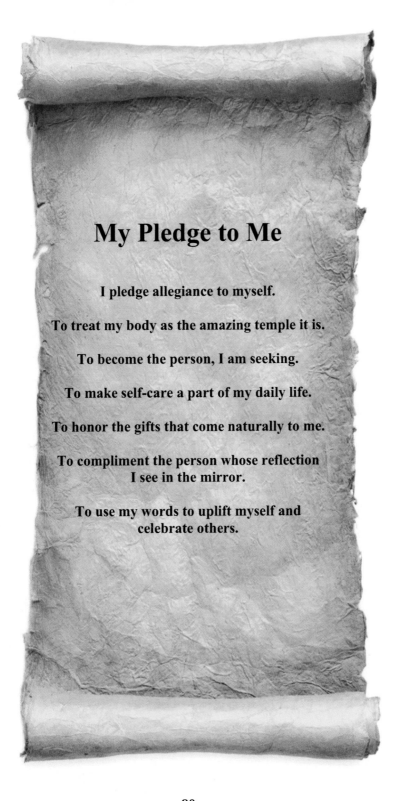

# My Pledge to Me

I pledge allegiance to myself.

To treat my body as the amazing temple it is.

To become the person, I am seeking.

To make self-care a part of my daily life.

To honor the gifts that come naturally to me.

To compliment the person whose reflection
I see in the mirror.

To use my words to uplift myself and
celebrate others.

# Change Cost.

# Value in Vulnerability

I have found the value in my vulnerability.

"Owning our story can be hard but not nearly as difficult as spending our lives running from it. Embracing our vulnerabilities is risky, but not nearly as dangerous as giving up on love and belonging and joy— the experiences that make us the most vulnerable. Only when we are brave enough to explore the darkness will we discover the infinite power of our light." — Brene' Brown

I'm in love again with who I am, and I am elated about who I am becoming. I view my vulnerability as a sign of my growth, courage, and care for my community. I feel my ascension and I give thanks for each of my teachers.

I give thanks for every self-care moment and journal entry. I feel my light shining brighter. I am energized by my ability to illuminate the path for another because of my choice to identify the value in my vulnerability. I believe, for our light to truly shine brightly, we must show up as our authentic selves.

It was a part of your path to pick up this book. It's time to rediscover who you are minus the expectations of others. When we don't address our concerns, it shows up in our decision making. Examine your concerns and your behavior patterns. Take responsibility for your part. We are all here to live and love, grow, and glow, and to serve and shine our light. Our lives and legacies matters, someone is depending on it.

# Self-Care For Success
## Legacy Wall

"If you're going to live, leave a legacy. Make a mark on the world that can't be erased."
– Maya Angelou

**In Memoriam:**
Frank & Theresa B. Jett
Laura M. Jett
Walter Roy
Clarisa B. Young
Karen Lynn Williams
Cleveland E. Smith, Sr.
Georgiana Pierce
Ernest M. Jett
Lawrence P. Jett
Anthony Dean
Willie Joe Dean, Sr.

**Legacy Living....**
Theresa Williams
Clarisa Smith
Gloria Dean
Aryana McKay
Laura Barker
Amanda Shaw
Brenda Kelley
Kim Martin-Raymond
Krystol Smith
Mr. & Mrs. Fletcher
Roneiko Henderson
Oscar Jones
Daniel Smith
Janene Hamilton
Michelle Smith
Courtney Bowman
Robyn Taylor
Shelly Scott
Alana Scott

Tashana Thompson
Tommy Smith
Sherall Fisher
Vivian Jackson
Detra Friley-Clark
Dannelle Crayton
Brittany Johnson
Chatele Chester
Venecia Wilburn
Pamela Lopez
Denise Dean
Tamara Brown
Phebee Sims
Sandie Porter
Felecia Garrison
Symone Fears
BreNita Jackson

*Blessings!*

# About The Writer

JoAnn Dean has been helping others gain clarity, elevate their confidence, and move into action for over 20 years!

She's known for being a trustworthy thought leader with a calm demeanor who over delivers. She privately empowers professional women to lead purposeful lives by focusing on the value of self-care, investing in, and putting themselves first. This leads to growing in areas they didn't anticipate, recapturing their power and decoding programming that no longer serves them.

JoAnn is the Founder of Inspired By JoAnn, LLC, a community created for the professional woman to pause from pouring into others, reconnect with herself, heal and embrace who she is through the support of Personal Life Coaching, Messages of Inspiration & The Exclusive Self-Care For Success Circle Membership Community.

She is a seven-time self-published author. She's a graduate of Southern University at New Orleans, where she obtained both a Bachelors & Master's Degree in Social Work. She is Board Certified Personal Life Coach. She is an alumnus of DeVos Urban Leadership Initiative and Life Purpose Institute where she obtained her Life Coaching Certification. JoAnn was featured in VoyageATL Magazine in 2019.

Her mantra: I give thanks for a perfect day. God is my unfailing supply. Miracles and signs follow me and wonders never cease. Divine love floods my consciousness. My mind is brilliant. My body is healthy. My spirit is tranquil. All is well. I am complete. And it is so.

Her mission is to create a community of 100 women with the focus of self-care, sisterhood, and spiritual growth.

# Experience her other work.

"The great use of life is to spend it for something that will outlast it."

~ William James

# Gratitude

When we are grateful, we recognize every moment as an opportunity for growth. Sometimes the gift is obvious, at other times we must seek deeper to capture its essence. Let gratitude become one of your teachers.

**Because of them, I AM.**
**Hugs & Blessings.**

Inspired By JoAnn, LLC, a community created for the professional woman to pause from pouring into others, reconnect with herself, heal, and embrace who she is through the support of Life Coaching, Messages of Inspiration & The Exclusive Self-Care for Success Membership Community.

## Stay Connected:

**Follow JoAnn**
Instagram @ Selfcare_For_Success
YouTube @ Selfcare_For_Success

To Book JoAnn for your next event go to www.joanndean.com

# Self-Care for Success!

## "Every Superwoman Needs a Support System!"

Together we discover and integrate new blueprints for the women we are becoming.

### Tell Your Story: Write a Book in 90 Days

Future generations will gain insight into who you are as they live out the legacy. After you're gone, your book will live on, telling your story in your words.

### One on One Coaching

Recapture your power lost in fear and early programming. Dive deeper into identifying the root cause of your limiting belief and blocks; find ways to work through them, creating the life you desire and the legacy you want to leave.

### The Self-Care for Success Circle

Professional women are welcomed into an intimate setting where we learn new ways of relating to ourselves, the world around us, and each other. We come together weekly with a circle of like-minded women, creating a sisterhood and unity, in a safe space where we can show up as ourselves.

## Join Our Community

### www.joanndean.com

# Living the Legacy!
## "This is that."

# Acknowledgment

Thank you to everyone who served as my teacher.

Until next time, continue to walk by faith and remember it all begins with you.
God bless.

Made in United States
Orlando, FL
16 January 2024

42384196R00066